STAR WARS®

THE STORY OF DARTH VADER

P9-CAB-614

Written by Catherine Saunders and Tori Kosara

Penguin Random House

Senior Editor Tori Kosara
Project Editor Lisa Stock
Editor Anant Sagar
Art Editor Pallavi Kapur
DTP Designer Umesh Singh Rawat
Pre-production Producer Siu Yin Chan
Pre-production Manager Sunil Sharma
Senior Producer Alex Bell
Managing Editors Sadie Smith, Chitra Subramanyam
Managing Art Editors Neha Ahuja, Ron Stobbart
Publisher Julie Ferris
Art Director Lisa Lanzarini
Publishing Director Simon Beecroft

Designed for DK by Mark Richards

For Lucasfilm
Executive Editor Jonathan W. Rinzler
Art Director Troy Alders
Story Group Rayne Roberts, Pablo Hidalgo, Leland Chee

Reading Consultant Linda B. Gambrell

First American Edition, 2015
Published in the United States by DK Publishing
345 Hudson Street, New York, New York 10014

Copyright © 2015 Dorling Kindersley Limited
A Penguin Random House Company
15 16 17 18 19 10 9 8 7 6 5 4 3 2
003-275293-Sep/15

© & TM 2015 LUCASFILM LTD.

All rights reserved.
Without limiting the rights under the copyright reserved above, no part of this publication may be reproduced, stored in or introduced into a retrieval system, or transmitted, in any form, or by any means (electronic, mechanical, photocopying, recording, or otherwise), without the prior written permission of the copyright owner.
Published in Great Britain by Dorling Kindersley Limited.

A catalog record for this book is available from the Library of Congress.
ISBN: 978-1-4654-3391-6 (Hardback)
ISBN: 978-1-4654-3392-3 (Paperback)

DK books are available at special discounts when purchased in bulk for sales promotions, premiums, fund-raising, or educational use. For details, contact: DK Publishing Special Markets, 345 Hudson Street, New York, New York 10014
SpecialSales@dk.com

Printed in the U.S.A.

A WORLD OF IDEAS:
SEE ALL THERE IS TO KNOW

www.starwars.com
www.dk.com

Contents

4 The story of Darth Vader
6 Two sides of the Force
8 Young Anakin Skywalker
10 A special calling
12 A new life begins
14 Meet Queen Amidala
16 Jedi training
18 Increasing frustration
20 Powerful friend
22 Unstoppable feelings
24 Turning to the dark side
26 Jedi heroes
28 Are you on a path to the dark side?
30 The dark side wins
32 The end of Anakin
34 The creation of Darth Vader
36 Building Darth Vader
38 Padmé's secret
40 The rise of Darth Vader
42 Civil war
44 Rebel victory
46 Imperial fleet
48 Star Destroyer
50 Vader's revenge
52 Cloud City
54 Like father, like son
56 Vader's choice
58 The death of Darth Vader
60 Glossary
61 Index

62 Guide for Parents

The story of Darth Vader

Take a look at Darth Vader—if you dare! He is a very dangerous man with many terrifying powers. Darth Vader is a ruthless Sith Lord who helps rule the galaxy for the evil Emperor Palpatine.

But Darth Vader was not always the masked Sith you see now. Once he was a talented Jedi Knight named Anakin Skywalker. Read on and uncover the story of how a promising young Jedi turned to the dark side of the Force.

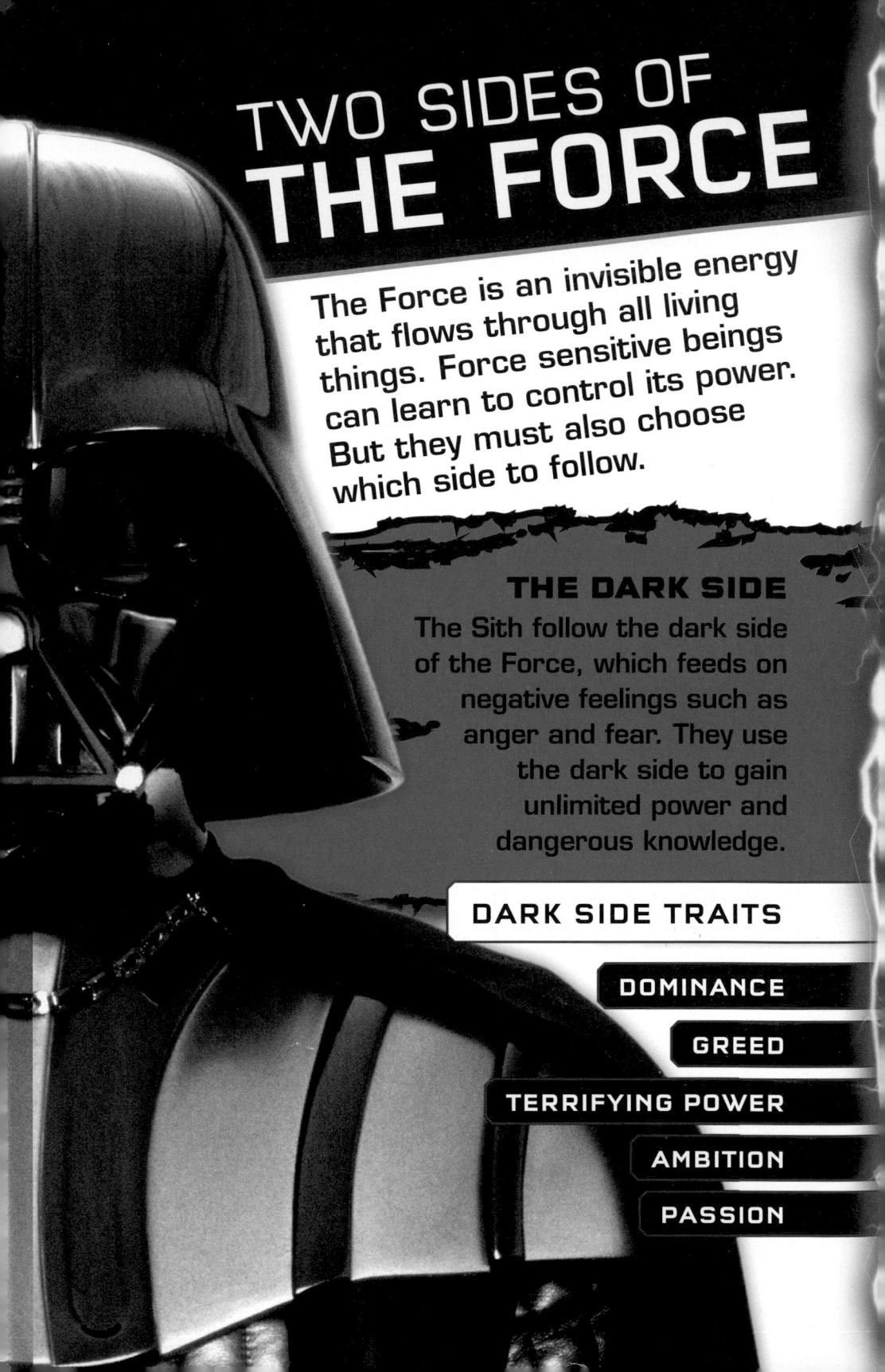

TWO SIDES OF THE FORCE

The Force is an invisible energy that flows through all living things. Force sensitive beings can learn to control its power. But they must also choose which side to follow.

THE DARK SIDE

The Sith follow the dark side of the Force, which feeds on negative feelings such as anger and fear. They use the dark side to gain unlimited power and dangerous knowledge.

DARK SIDE TRAITS

- DOMINANCE
- GREED
- TERRIFYING POWER
- AMBITION
- PASSION

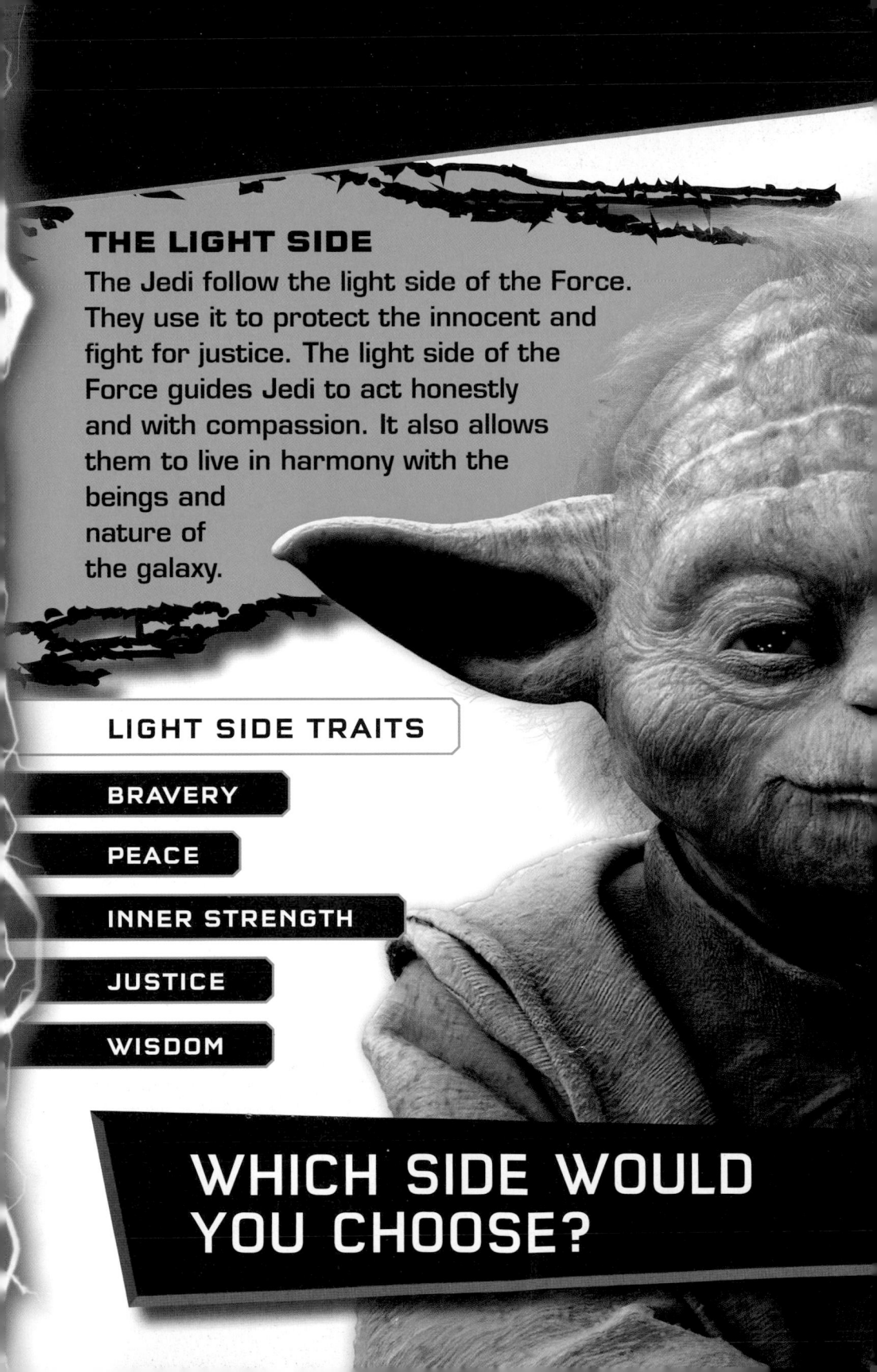

THE LIGHT SIDE

The Jedi follow the light side of the Force. They use it to protect the innocent and fight for justice. The light side of the Force guides Jedi to act honestly and with compassion. It also allows them to live in harmony with the beings and nature of the galaxy.

LIGHT SIDE TRAITS

- BRAVERY
- PEACE
- INNER STRENGTH
- JUSTICE
- WISDOM

WHICH SIDE WOULD YOU CHOOSE?

Young Anakin Skywalker

Anakin Skywalker grew up a slave on the desert planet Tatooine. His mother Shmi could not explain how Anakin came to be born—he had no father.

Anakin was a gentle child and he loved his mother very much. From a young age he was skilled at making and fixing mechanical things. When he was nine years old he built a droid named C-3PO to help his mother. However, Anakin was impulsive and liked to take risks.

A special calling

When Jedi Qui-Gon Jinn and Obi-Wan Kenobi landed on Tatooine to repair their ship, they met Anakin Skywalker. Qui-Gon realized Anakin had the potential to be a great Jedi. Anakin offered to enter a dangerous Podrace for Qui-Gon.

The Jedi Knight seized the opportunity to win the parts he needed for his ship and Anakin's freedom. He was sure that Anakin's Force powers would help him to win the race. He was right. Freed from slavery, Anakin was able to leave Tatooine with the Jedi, but first he had to say goodbye to his mother.

A new life begins

After leaving Tatooine, Qui-Gon asked the Jedi Council to let Anakin become his apprentice, but it refused. The Council thought that Anakin was already too old, and some wise members also sensed danger in Anakin's future.

Anakin and the Jedi liberated the planet Naboo from the Trade Federation invasion. When Anakin destroyed the Trade Federation's Droid Control Ship, the Jedi Council changed its mind. Although Qui-Gon had been killed by a Sith, Obi-Wan promised to train Anakin instead.

Meet Queen Amidala

The young queen of Naboo is a very popular leader. Not only is she brave and loyal, she is also an expert with a blaster!

Regal Ruler
Royal jewel of Zenda
Gold faceframes
Hem made from potolli fur
Intricate gold embroidery
Glowing Sein jewel

Jedi training

Anakin Skywalker returned to the Jedi Temple on the capital planet Coruscant to begin his training. He was taught how to use and control his incredible Force powers. Anakin was also instructed in the ways of the Jedi Knights. Jedi must not be governed by emotions. They are peace-loving, calm, and use their skills only to defend, never to attack.

As Jedi Master Obi-Wan Kenobi's Padawan learner or apprentice, Anakin came to view Obi-Wan as the closest thing he had to a father figure.

Increasing frustration

Anakin loved and respected Obi-Wan, but often felt frustrated by him. Anakin was confident in his Jedi abilities, and felt that Obi-Wan was holding him back. He was tired of being just a Padawan.

Obi-Wan knew that Anakin had the potential to be a powerful Jedi Knight.

But he also believed that Anakin had not yet mastered his emotions, as a Jedi should. Obi-Wan was proved right when Anakin was reunited with Padmé Amidala after ten years. The feelings that Anakin had felt for her as a boy had not gone away. Soon he would no longer be able to control them.

Powerful friend

The galaxy was formed as a Republic, which meant that it was ruled by a Senate in which all the planets had representatives. As his frustration grew, Anakin found himself turning to Chancellor Palpatine, leader of the Republic.

Palpatine seemed to understand how Anakin felt. He was a good listener. Anakin believed that Palpatine was on his side, unlike Obi-Wan. Anakin did not realize that Palpatine was trying to destroy the Republic and seize power for himself.

Unstoppable feelings

Palpatine's sinister influence increased Anakin's frustration with Obi-Wan and the Jedi Order. He was feeling very confused. When he was chosen to escort Padmé back to Naboo, he finally lost the battle to control his feelings for her.

Padmé was now a Senator and had a duty to the Republic, but she too could not prevent herself from falling in love with Anakin. They were secretly married on Naboo. Jedi were not supposed to get emotionally attached to others. Anakin had broken the rules, but he didn't care.

Turning to the dark side

Anakin had not forgotten his mother Shmi, whom he had left on Tatooine. He began to have terrible nightmares about her, so he went to find her.

Anakin went back to Tatooine. There he discovered that Shmi had married a farmer named Cliegg Lars, who had freed her from slavery.

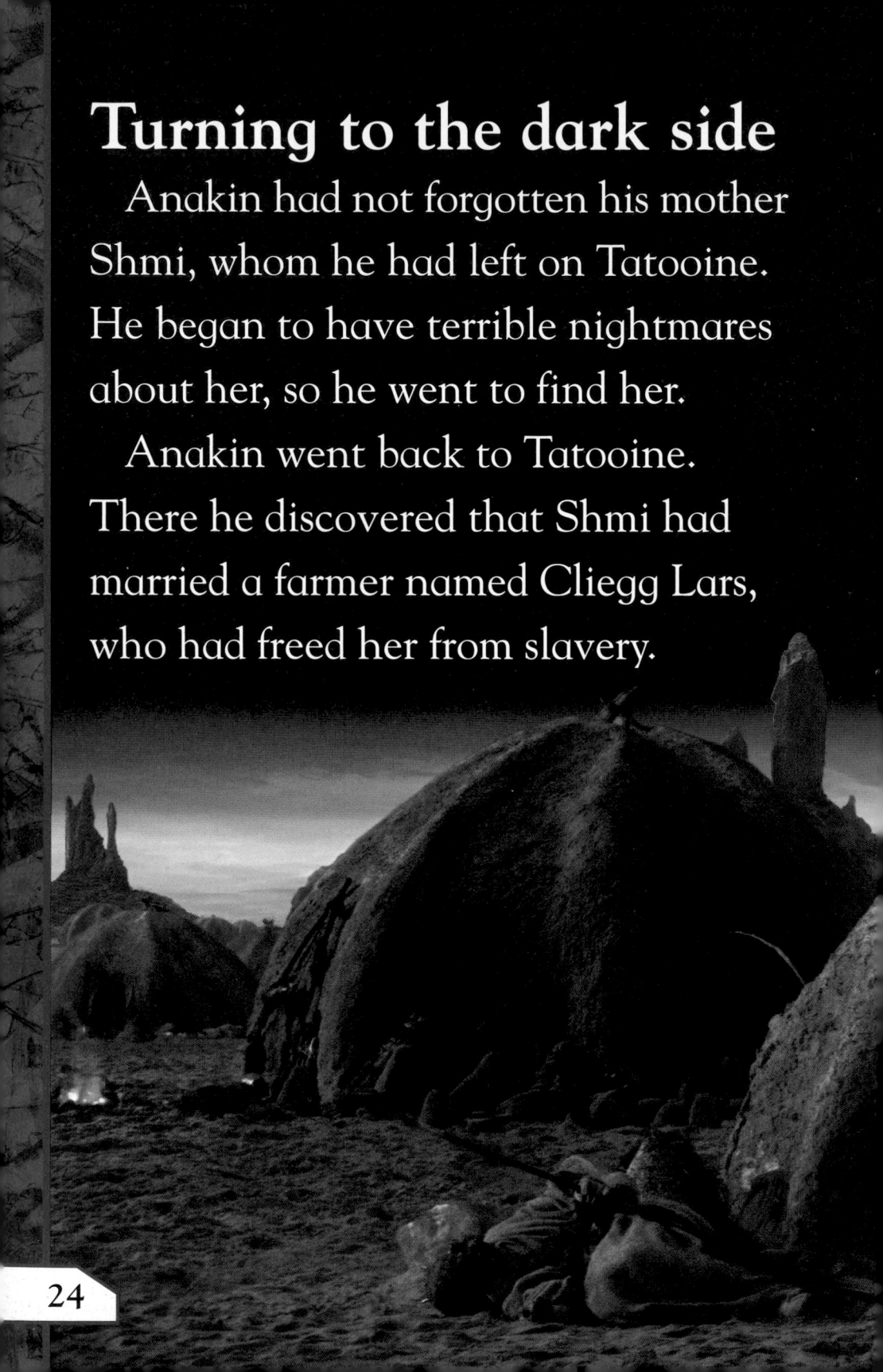

Anakin also learned that his mother had been kidnapped by Sand People. He went in search of her but he was too late and she died in his arms. Overcome with grief and anger, Anakin took revenge on the Sand People.

Jedi heroes

Although he was increasingly ruled by his emotions, Anakin had not yet fully turned to the dark side. When the Republic was forced into the Clone Wars, Anakin fought bravely with the Jedi.

The Clone Wars lasted for many years and Anakin and Obi-Wan became famous heroes.

Anakin felt truly alive in the heat of the battle and his powers became even stronger. However, Anakin still felt that he was being held back by the Jedi and that only Palpatine was encouraging his talents. He felt that maybe the Jedi teachings were not right and that greater power lay elsewhere.

ARE YOU ON A PATH TO THE DARK SIDE?

Every decision has an effect. A single moment is all it takes to choose between the light side and the dark side. Now the choice is yours: Which path will you take?

START HERE

Can you control your emotions?

YES

Is friendship more important than success?

NO

Would you try to negotiate before entering a battle?

NO

Is strength better than emotional intelligence?

NO

YES

Do you ever go back on your word?

YES

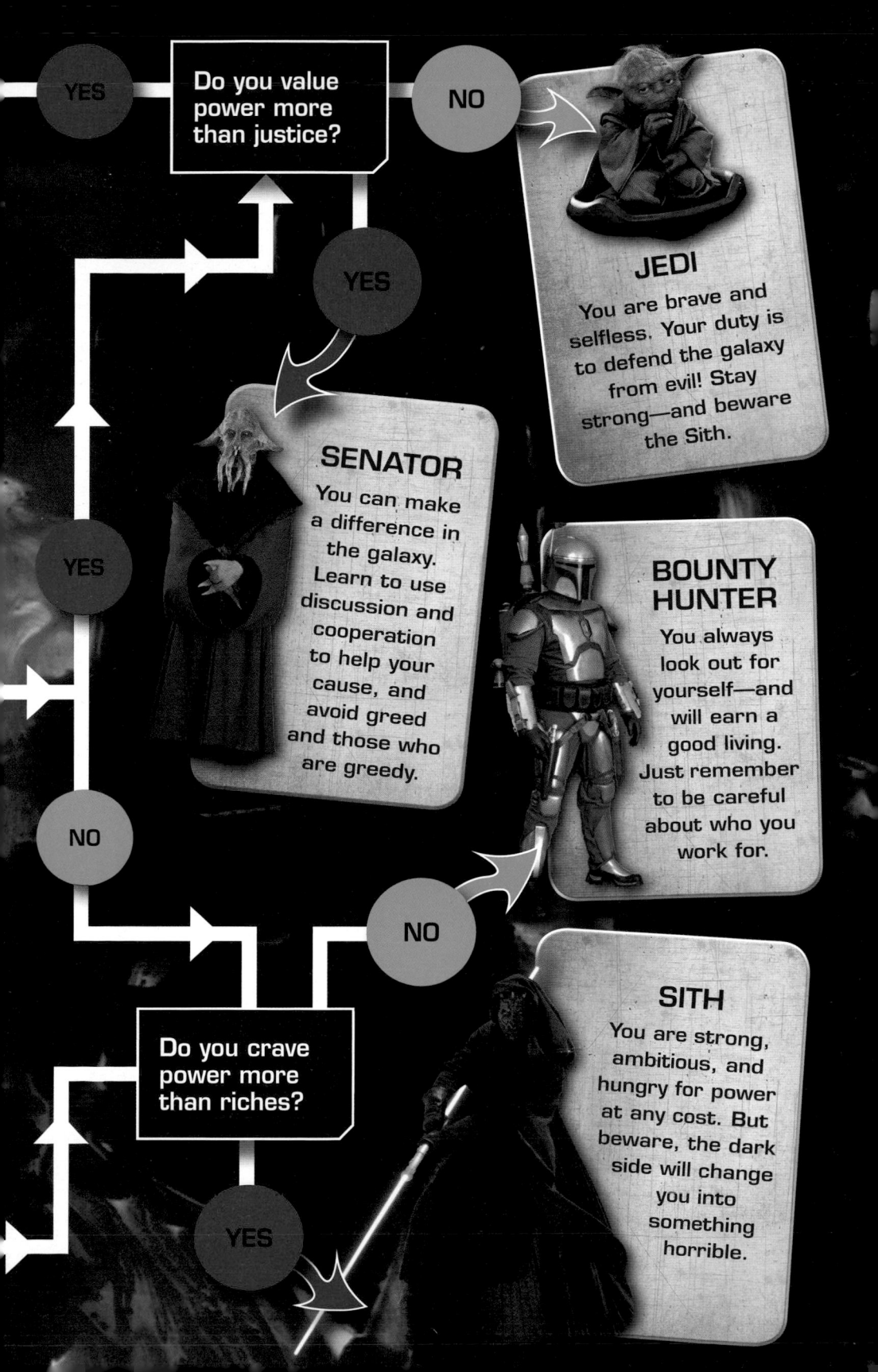
Do you value power more than justice?
YES
NO
JEDI
You are brave and selfless. Your duty is to defend the galaxy from evil! Stay strong—and beware the Sith.
YES
SENATOR
You can make a difference in the galaxy. Learn to use discussion and cooperation to help your cause, and avoid greed and those who are greedy.
YES
NO
BOUNTY HUNTER
You always look out for yourself—and will earn a good living. Just remember to be careful about who you work for.
NO
Do you crave power more than riches?
YES
SITH
You are strong, ambitious, and hungry for power at any cost. But beware, the dark side will change you into something horrible.

The dark side wins

Toward the end of the Clone Wars, Palpatine was kidnapped. Anakin and Obi-Wan went to his aid, but it was a trap. Sith Lord Count Dooku was waiting for them. He knocked out Obi-Wan and began to fight Anakin.

Palpatine urged Anakin to kill Dooku and Anakin gave in.

A short time later Anakin chose Palpatine over the Jedi and his transition to the dark side was complete. He knelt before Palpatine—his new Sith Master.

The end of Anakin

Anakin turned his back on the Jedi and adopted the Sith name Darth Vader. On Palpatine's orders he set out to destroy his former friends and comrades. Darth Vader also became convinced that Padmé and Obi-Wan were plotting against him. He nearly killed his wife and then faced Obi-Wan in an intense lightsaber battle.

Although Darth Vader was driven by anger and the power of the dark side, Obi-Wan won the terrible fight. Vader suffered horrific injuries and burns.

The creation of Darth Vader

Although Darth Vader's body seemed beyond repair, Palpatine refused to give up on his evil apprentice. He took Vader's body to a secret medical facility where it was rebuilt using cyber-technology. Vader needed special breathing equipment and life-support systems just to stay alive.

Behind the black armor and a black helmet, it seemed that no part of the human Anakin Skywalker was left. Darth Vader had given himself completely to the ways of the dark side.

BUILDING DARTH VADER

Saving the life of the new Sith apprentice was no easy task.

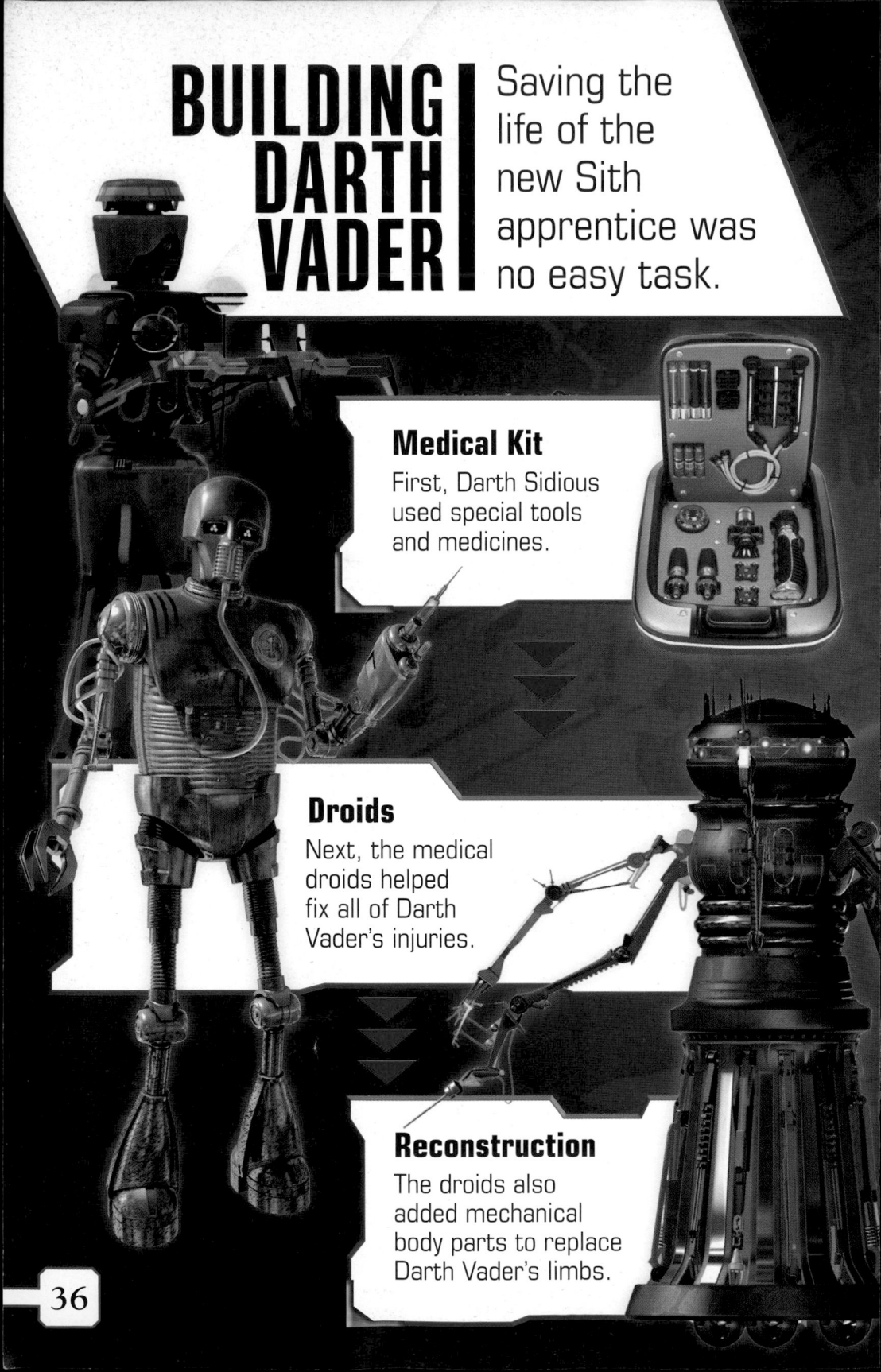

Medical Kit

First, Darth Sidious used special tools and medicines.

Droids

Next, the medical droids helped fix all of Darth Vader's injuries.

Reconstruction

The droids also added mechanical body parts to replace Darth Vader's limbs.

Armor
Finally, Darth Vader was covered in strong black armor to protect his body.
Helmet
Allows Vader to breathe and protects his face
Chest control box
Monitors Darth Vader's life support
Belt control panel
Regulates armor temperature

Padmé's secret

With her husband lost to the dark side, a heartbroken Padmé gave birth to twins, whom she named Luke and Leia. Loyal Jedi Master Obi-Wan Kenobi was by her side, but Padmé had no will to live without Anakin.

Jedi Master Yoda decided to keep the children a secret from their father. Obi-Wan took Luke to Tatooine to live with Shmi Skywalker's stepson, Owen Lars, and his wife, Beru.

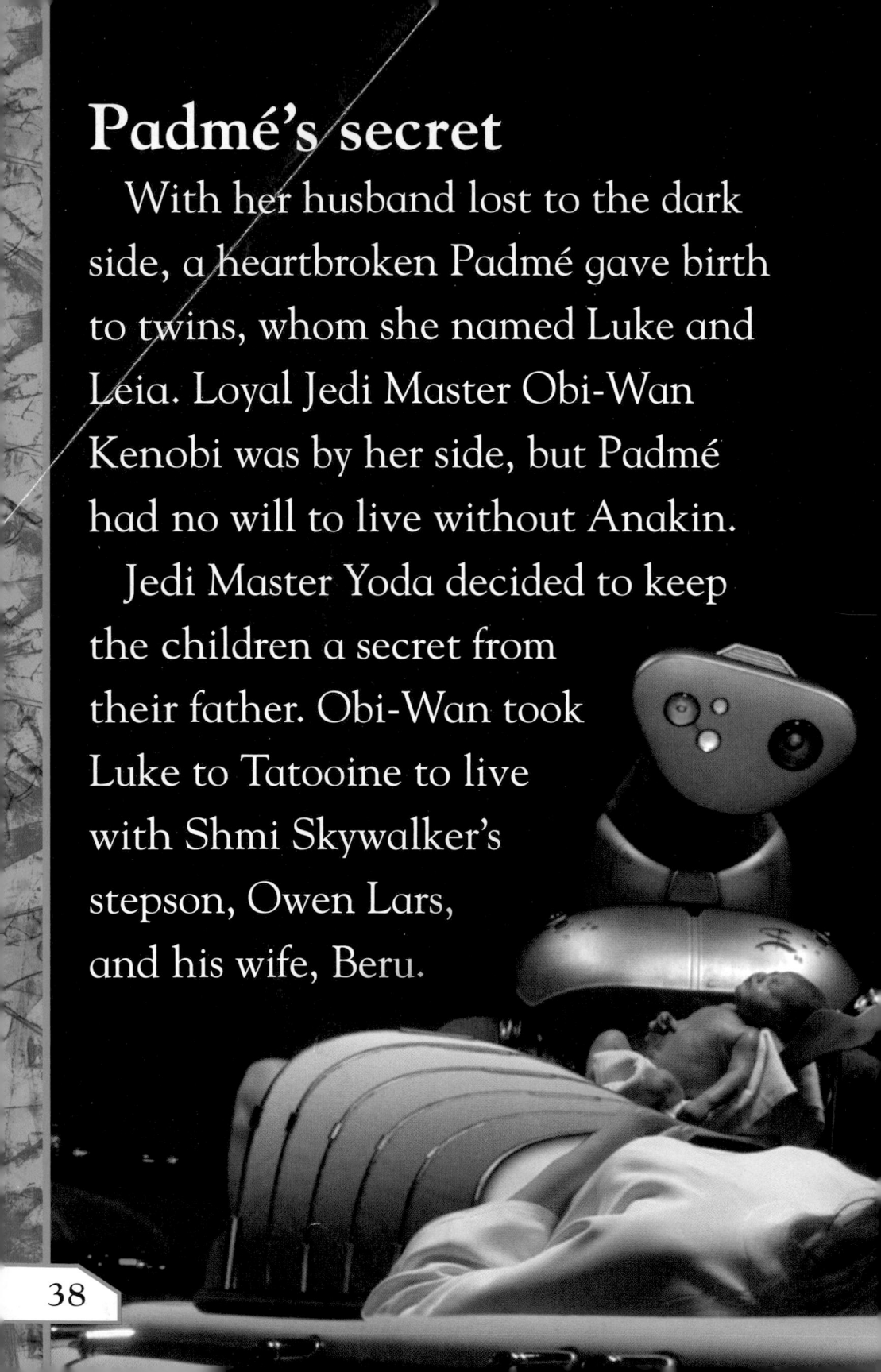

Luke's life on the desert planet was hard and lonely. Leia, was taken to the planet Alderaan. She was adopted by Obi-Wan's friend Bail Organa and brought up a princess. Neither twin knew that the other existed. They did not suspect that their father was the feared Sith Lord Vader.

The rise of Darth Vader

The Republic had been destroyed and the evil Palpatine ruled the galaxy as Emperor, with Darth Vader by his side. The Sith Lords would let nothing and no one stand in their way. Vader's terrifying appearance, deep voice, and loud artificial breathing struck fear into the hearts of his enemies and allies alike. Even his own generals could not escape Vader's wrath and, as time went by, the Sith's powers grew even stronger.

Anakin Skywalker had been a brave pilot and skilled with a lightsaber, but the dark side of the Force continued to corrupt Darth Vader. He strangled people using the Force and could read the thoughts of others.

Civil war

Although the Sith had destroyed the Republic and most of the Jedi, a small group of rebels bravely opposed the Empire. Known as the Rebel Alliance, they were based on the planet Yavin 4. Little did Darth Vader know that two of the rebels were his children, Luke and Leia.

The famous Jedi Master Obi-Wan Kenobi faced his former apprentice once again.

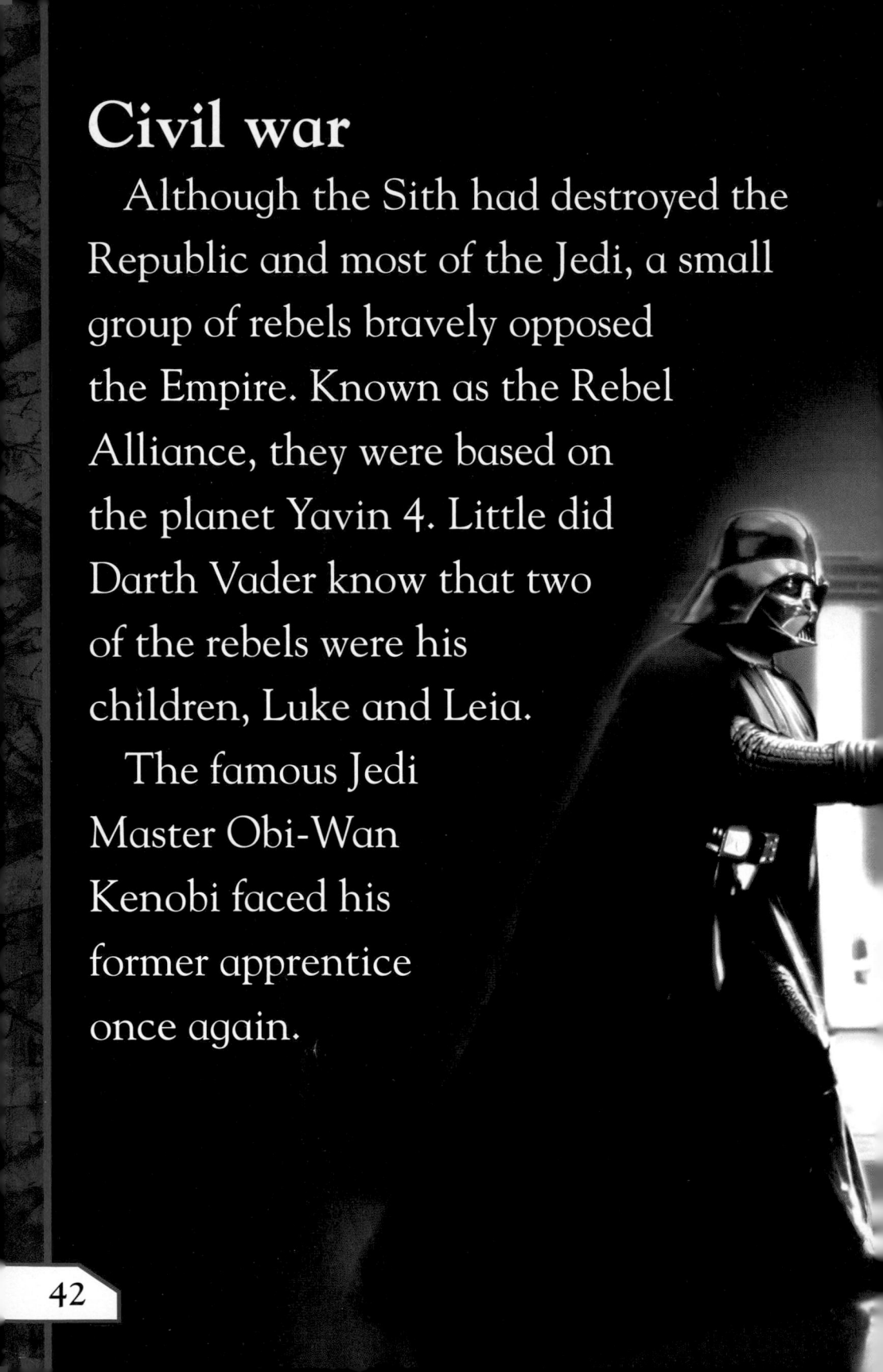

This time Obi-Wan let Darth Vader win in order to show Luke that, thanks to the Force, a person's spirit continues after death.

Rebel victory

The Emperor decided to build a superweapon known as a Death Star. It was the size of a small moon and had the power to blow up entire planets.

However, the rebels managed to obtain the plans for the weapon and learned that it had a fatal flaw. One exhaust port was unprotected and if a pilot fired torpedoes into its shaft, a chain reaction of explosions would destroy the whole Death Star. The rebels sent a squadron of star fighters and their best pilot, Luke Skywalker, had one chance to destroy the Death Star.
He did not miss.

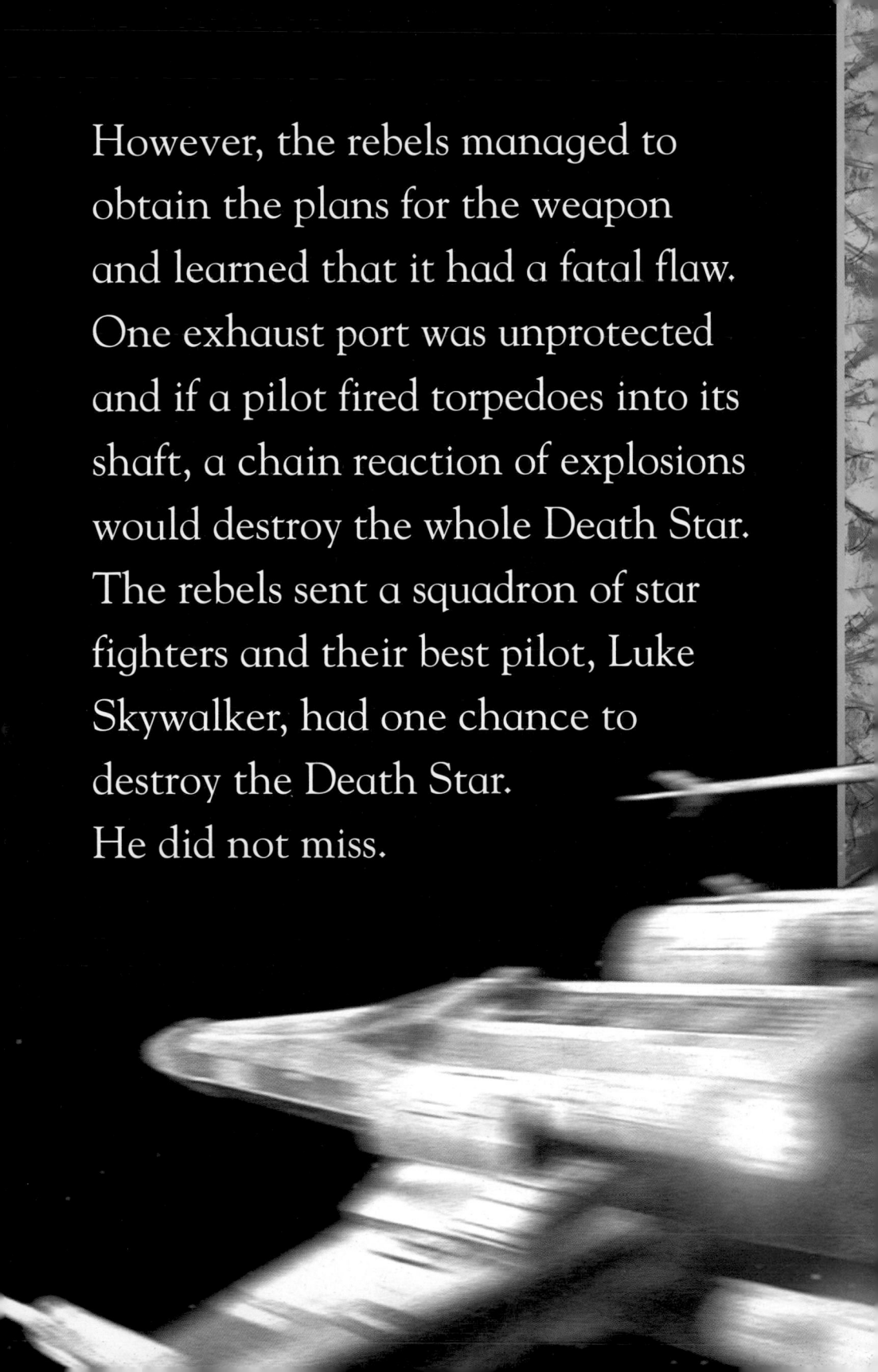

Imperial fleet

The Rebel Alliance had only a small number of ships which already bore the scars of previous battles, but the Empire had a massive fleet of starships. The largest and most powerful Imperial vessels were known as Super Star Destroyers. Powered by 13 engines, the Super Star Destroyers were arrow shaped and loaded with deadly weapons.

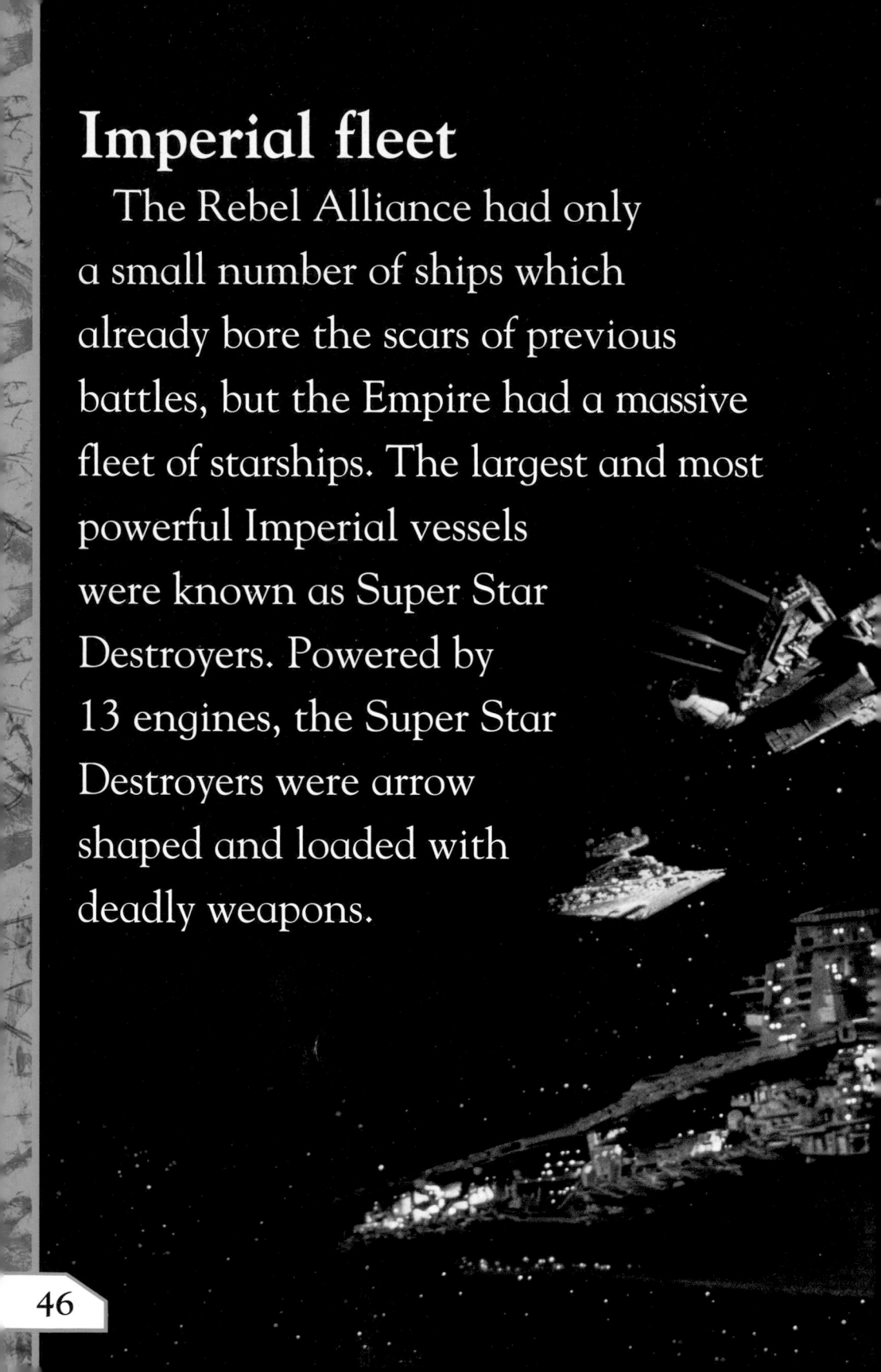

Darth Vader's ship *Executor* was the most powerful Super Star Destroyer. Vader commanded the fleet, but the Emperor gave his orders via hologram.

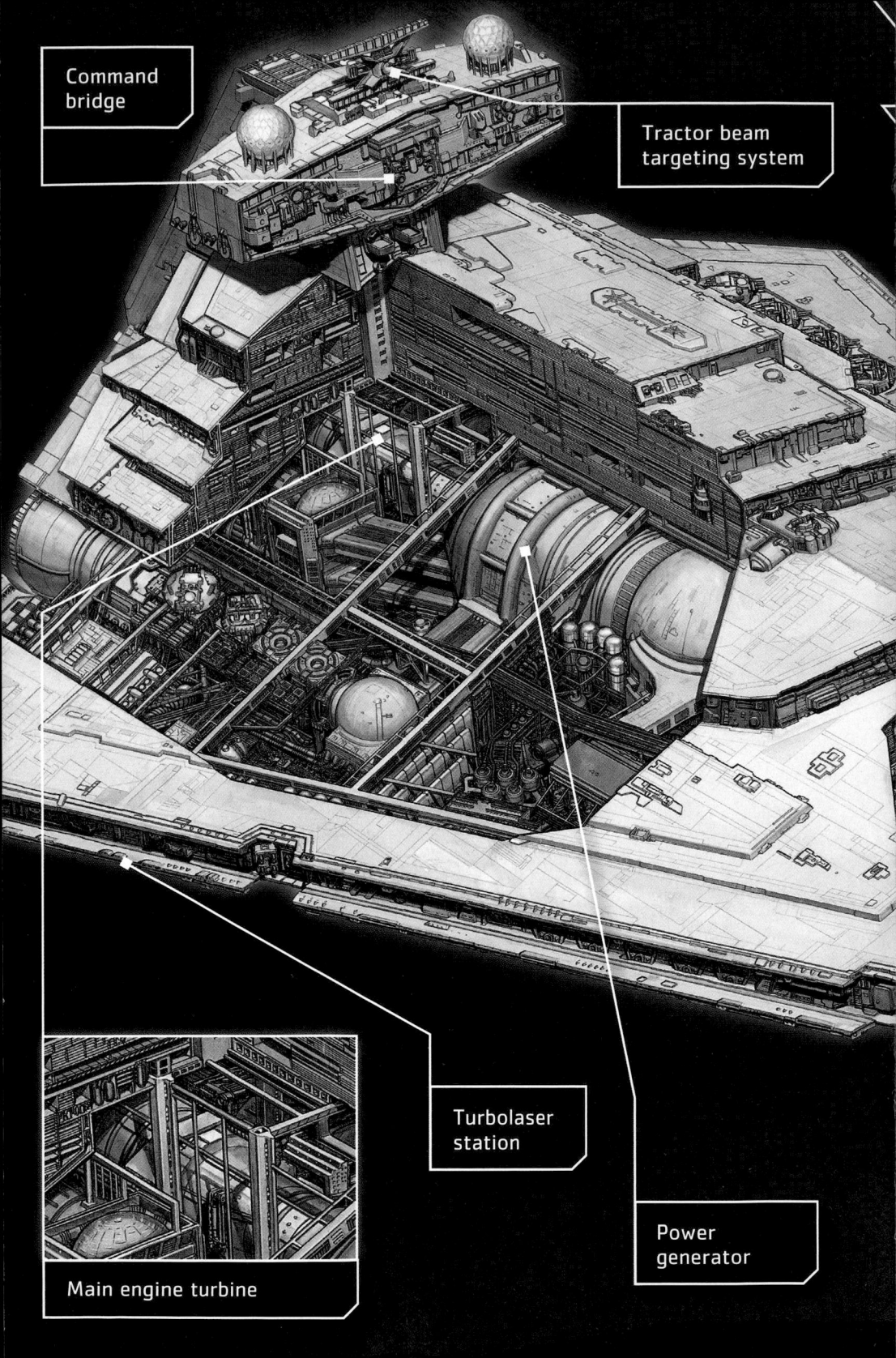
Command bridge
Tractor beam targeting system
Turbolaser station
Power generator
Main engine turbine

STAR DESTROYER

The Star Destroyer is a symbol of the Empire's military might. It carries powerful weapons and armies across the galaxy to fight those who oppose the Imperial rule.

Vader's revenge

When the rebels blew up the first Death Star, it made Darth Vader and the Emperor extremely angry. They began building a new Death Star, and Darth Vader set out to find and destroy the rebels responsible.

Vader sent probe droids to every corner of the galaxy to find the rebels' new base. He finally located them on the ice planet Hoth.

The Sith Lord traveled to Hoth with the Imperial fleet and launched a deadly attack. The rebels had to evacuate very quickly and their forces were scattered far and wide across the galaxy.

Cloud City

Emperor Palpatine had finally told Darth Vader the truth about Luke Skywalker. As Darth Vader laid a trap for Luke on Cloud City, he was looking for more than just a troublesome rebel—he was searching for his son.

As Luke and Vader fought with lightsabers, Luke still had no idea who lay behind Darth Vader's mask. The fight ended when Vader chopped off Luke's hand. He revealed that he was Luke's father and asked his son to join him and rule the galaxy. Despite his painful wound, Luke was strong with the Force. He refused to turn to the dark side.

LIKE FATHER, LIKE SON

In many ways, the lives of Anakin and Luke Skywalker have followed similar paths.

LATE TO THE JEDI ORDER

Nine-year-old Anakin is a lot older than most children who begin their Jedi training.

Luke begins his Jedi training when he is 22 years old—much older than any Padawan before him.

VERY STRONG IN THE FORCE

Anakin's Force skills help him pilot his spaceship at incredible speeds.

Luke uses his Jedi reflexes to pilot his spaceship and destroy the Death Star.

DISOBEDIENT

Anakin ignores many Jedi teachings, including the rule that a Jedi must not become overly attached to others.

Luke does not take Yoda's advice about completing his Jedi training. He runs off to help his friends.

SCARRED IN BATTLE

Anakin loses his right hand during a duel with Darth Tyranus. It reminds him of his inexperience.

Darth Vader cuts off Luke's right hand in a duel. It reminds Luke of his similarity to his father.

"I AM A JEDI, LIKE MY FATHER BEFORE ME."

Luke Skywalker

Vader's choice

For many years, Darth Vader had been loyal to Emperor Palpatine. However, meeting his son Luke—a good and true person—seemed to change him. Could it be that some part of Anakin Skywalker remained behind Vader's mask?

Palpatine had predicted that Luke would come to them and he would be turned to the dark side. When Luke surrendered, it seemed that Palpatine would be proved right. As father and son fought once more, Luke felt anger and hatred and drew close to the dark side.

At the last moment Luke was able to control his feelings and refused to join the dark side. As an enraged Palpatine attacked Luke, Anakin Skywalker finally returned from the dark side to save his son.

The death of Darth Vader

At the vital moment, Darth Vader returned from his nightmare. Luke had reminded him that he was once a great Jedi named Anakin Skywalker. However, as Vader saved his son, he was fatally wounded by the Emperor.

As Anakin lay dying, he asked Luke to remove his helmet so that he could look at his son's face with his own eyes. When Anakin died, his body disappeared into the light side of the Force. Luke was sad that his father was dead but proud of him, too. The light side of the Force had overcome the dark side and Anakin Skywalker had returned.

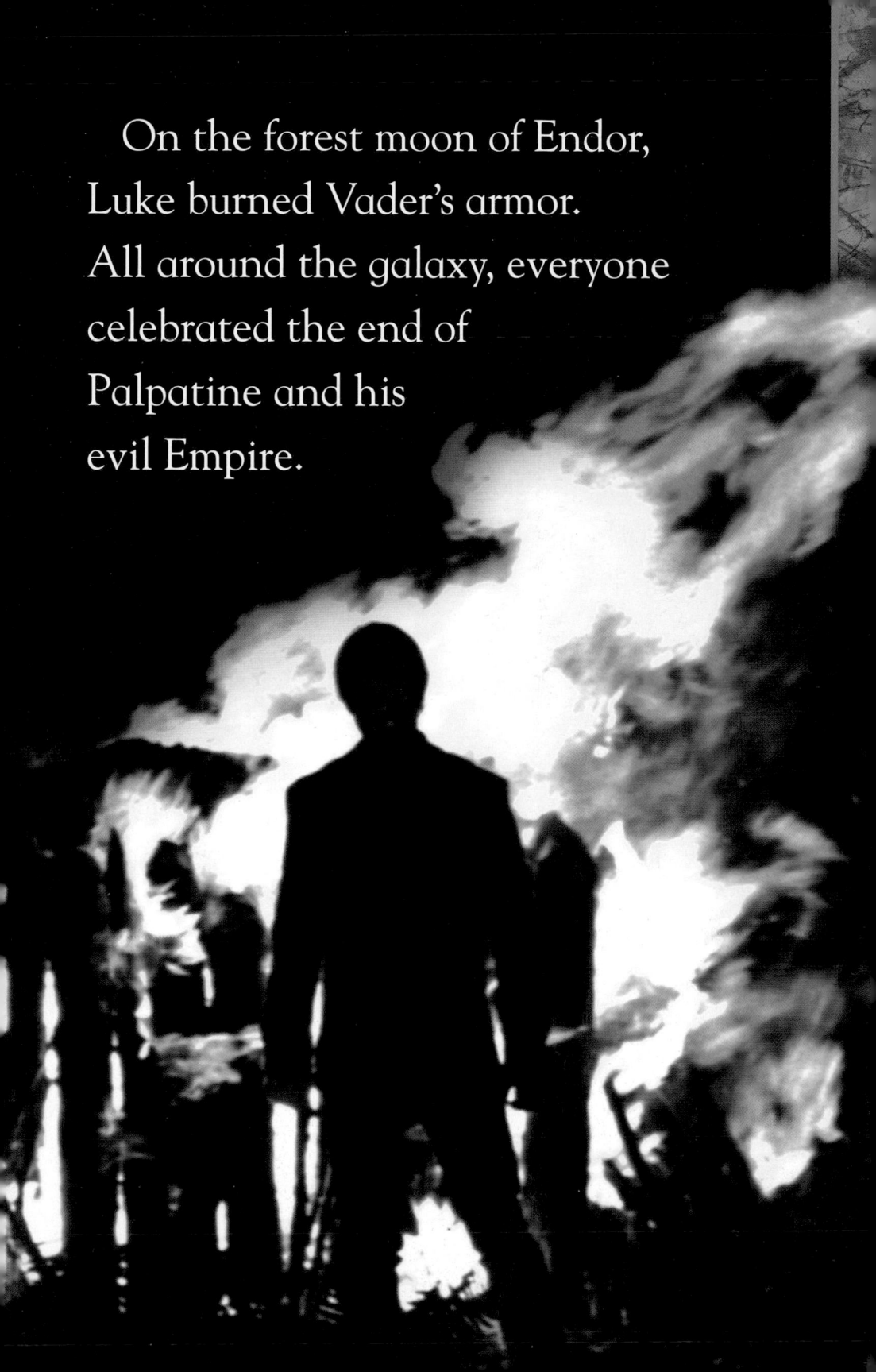

On the forest moon of Endor, Luke burned Vader's armor. All around the galaxy, everyone celebrated the end of Palpatine and his evil Empire.

Glossary

Grief
Very strong feeling of sadness.

Jedi Knight
A warrior with special powers who defends the galaxy from evil.

Liberated
To be free from the control of a person, group, or government.

Lightsaber
A Jedi and Sith weapon, made of glowing energy.

Rebel
Someone who opposes whoever is in power.

Representatives
People chosen to act or speak for others.

Sinister
Giving a feeling that something evil or bad is happening or could happen.

Index

Anakin Skywalker 5, 8–9, 10–11, 12–13, 16, 18–19, 20–21, 22–23, 24–25, 26–27, 30–31, 32–33, 34, 38, 41, 54–55, 56–57, 58

apprentice 12, 16, 34, 36, 42

dark side 5, 6, 24–25, 26, 28–29, 30–31, 33, 34, 38, 41, 53, 56–57, 58

Darth Sidious 36

Darth Vader 4–5, 33, 34–35, 36–37, 39, 40–41, 42–43, 47, 50, 51, 52–53, 55, 56–57, 58–59

Death Star 44–45, 50, 54

Emperor 5, 41, 44, 47, 50, 52, 56, 58

Force 5, 6–7, 11, 16, 41, 43, 53, 54, 58

galaxy 5, 7, 20, 29, 41, 49, 51, 53, 59

Jedi 5, 7, 10–11, 12–13, 16–17, 18–19, 22–23, 26–27, 29, 31, 33, 38, 42, 54–55, 58

lightsaber 33, 41, 53

Luke Skywalker 38–39, 42–43, 45, 52–53, 54–55, 56–57, 58–59

Naboo 13, 14, 22–23

Obi-Wan Kenobi 10, 13, 16, 18–19, 21, 22, 26, 30, 33, 38–39, 42–43

Padawan 16, 18, 54

Padmé Amidala 14–15, 19, 22–23, 33, 38–39

Palpatine 5, 20–21, 22, 27, 30–31, 33, 34, 41, 52, 56–57, 59

Princess Leia 38–39, 42

Qui-Gon Jinn 10, 12–13

Rebel Alliance 42, 46

rebels 42, 45, 50–51, 52

Republic 14, 20–21, 23, 26, 41, 42

Sith 5, 6, 13, 29, 30–31, 33, 36, 39, 41, 42, 51

Tatooine 8, 10–11, 12, 24, 38

Guide for Parents

DK Readers is a four-level interactive reading adventure series for children, developing the habit of reading widely for both pleasure and information. These books have an exciting main narrative interspersed with a range of reading genres to suit your child's reading ability, as required by the Common Core State Standards. Each book is designed to develop your child's reading skills, fluency, grammar awareness, and comprehension in order to build confidence and engagement when reading.

Ready for a *Reading Alone* book

YOUR CHILD SHOULD

- be able to read most words without needing to stop and break them down into sound parts.
- read smoothly, in phrases and with expression. By this level, your child will be mostly reading silently.
- self-correct when some word or sentence doesn't sound right.

A Valuable and Shared Reading Experience

For some children, text reading, particularly nonfiction, requires much effort, but adult participation can make this both fun and easier. So here are a few tips on how to use this book with your child.

TIP 1 Check out the contents together before your child begins:

- Invite your child to check the blurb, contents page, and layout of the book and comment on it.
- Ask your child to make predictions about the story.
- Talk about the information your child might want to find out.

TIP 2 Encourage fluent and flexible reading:

- Support your child to read in fluent, expressive phrases, making full use of punctuation and thinking about the meaning.

- Encourage your child to slow down and check information where appropriate.

TIP 3 Indicators that your child is reading for meaning:

- Your child will be responding to the text if he/she is self-correcting and varying his/her voice.
- Your child will want to talk about what he/she is reading or is eager to turn the page to find out what will happen next.

TIP 4 Share and discuss:

- Encourage your child to recall specific details after each chapter.
- Provide opportunities for your child to pick out interesting words and discuss what they mean.
- Discuss how the author captures the reader's interest, or how effective the nonfiction layouts are.
- Ask questions about the text. These help develop comprehension skills and awareness of the language used.

A FEW ADDITIONAL TIPS

- Read to your child regularly to demonstrate fluency, phrasing, and expression; to find out or check information; and for sharing enjoyment.
- Encourage your child to reread favorite texts to increase reading confidence and fluency.
- Check that your child is reading a range of different types of material, such as poems, jokes, and following instructions.

- Series consultant, **Dr. Linda Gambrell**, Distinguished Professor of Education at Clemson University, has served as President of the National Reading Conference, the College Reading Association, and the International Reading Association. She is also reading consultant for the **DK Adventures.**

Have you read these other great books from DK?

READING ALONE 3

Test what makes rockets fly. Which design would you use?

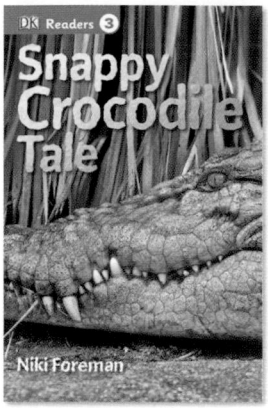

Follow Chris Croc's adventures from a baby to king of the river.

© 2015 Lucasfilm Ltd and ™

Join the heroes of the rebellion as they continue to fight the Empire.

© 2015 Lucasfilm Ltd and ™

Learn all about Yoda's battles and how he uses the Force.

© 2015 The LEGO Group and © 2015 Lucasfilm Ltd and ™

Can Luke Skywalker help the rebels defeat the evil Empire?

© 2015 The LEGO Group

Meet the heroes of Chima™ and help them find the Legend Beasts.